NAVIGATING YOUR NEW YORK
HIGH NET WORTH
DIVORCE

David I. Bliven

Copyright © 2021 by David I. Bliven.

All rights reserved. No part of this publication may be reproduced, distributed, or transmitted in any form or by any means, including photocopying, recording, or other electronic or mechanical methods, without the prior written permission of the publisher, except in the case of brief quotations embodied in critical reviews and certain other noncommercial uses permitted by copyright law. For permission requests, write to the publisher, addressed "Attention: Permissions Coordinator," at the address below.

Jacobs & Whitehall
73-03 Bell Blvd, #10
Oakland Gardens, NY 11364
www.jacobsandwhitehall.com
(888) 991-2766

Ordering Information:

Quantity sales. Special discounts are available on quantity purchases by corporations, associations, and others. For details, contact the publisher at the address above.

Orders by U.S. trade bookstores and wholesalers. Please contact Jacobs & Whitehall: Tel: (888) 991-2766 or visit www.jacobsandwhitehall.com.

Printed in the United States of America

Published in 2021

ISBN: 978-1-954506-01-5

FOREWORD

Contrary to common perceptions, having a high income or high net worth does not insulate oneself from problems – indeed, having more money may actually increase the likelihood to get divorced[1].

Indeed, while infidelity is still amongst the leading reasons why people get divorced, fighting over money is also one of the frequently cited reasons why people do not remain married[2]. Some articles have cited "money" as the leading reason why people get divorced (as the above article states), while others list it as "the leading reason" in roughly 36% of divorces[3].

---

[1] https://www.cnbc.com/2018/10/10/being-rich-may-increase-your-odds-of-divorce.html#:~:text=The%20more%20you%20earn%2C%20the,American%20Academy%20of%20Matrimonial%20Lawyers.

[2] https://www.cnbc.com/2015/02/04/money-is-the-leading-cause-of-stress-in-relationships.html

[3] https://www.insider.com/why-people-get-divorced-2019-1

Likewise, if one is a celebrity, one is that much more likely to get divorced vis-à-vis the general population[4].

That said, the question becomes: am I considered "high income" or "high net worth?" If you're not, then this book really isn't for you (no offense) and I recommend my book "Navigating Your New York Divorce Case."

Definitions of "high net worth" abound, but one working definition includes those with a net worth of at least $1 million[5]. The cited article goes on to cite 3 helpful measures of "high net worth" or "high income":

- Income (of at least $250,000 or greater)
- Investable assets/investments (of at least $500,000)
- Net worth ($1 million or more)

---

[4] https://www.securitylawbrief.com/is-celebrity-divorce-common/

[5]https://www.fidelity.com/news/article/default/202010121602BANKRATEBANKRATE433402382#:~:text=Typically%2C%20a%20high%2Dnet%2D,with%20a%20wealth%20management%20firm.

4

And while that category would seem relatively small – it's not. In New York City, nearly a million people have net worths of at least $1 million[6]. And New York City ranked only 2d as of 2017 in the number of "ultra high net worth" individuals – those having net worths of at least $30 million[7]. Indeed, Westchester County alone has nearly 8,000 millionaires[8], though then tend to be clustered in particular neighborhoods[9].

One may also wonder: what's net worth? Put simply: net worth is assets minus debt. One simply adds up all the items of value (properties, investments,

---

[6] https://www.cnbc.com/2019/01/18/new-york-city-has-more-millionaires-than-any-other-city-in-the-world.html

[7] https://www.cnbc.com/2018/09/14/the-richest-cities-in-the-world.html

[8] https://www.lohud.com/story/news/politics/politics-on-the-hudson/2019/03/15/million-dollar-earners-new-york-fell-concern-grows-over-taxes/3153657002/

[9] https://www.recordonline.com/story/news/2020/03/02/westchester-leads-country-with-wealthiest-communities/111829602/

retirement, money in the bank) and subtracts debt (often in the case of the lower-rung of high net worth individuals, that's usually just mortgage(s)).

In any event, if you're a person who fits the above definitions, then you're high income or high net worth – most likely both. And this is so even if you think of yourself as "upper-middle class.[10]"

The point of this book, however, is that while you may be high income or high net worth, divorce is different than the "average Joe." First, there's affordability – even "average" divorces cost around $15,000 – a sum unaffordable to many persons earning under median income[11]. Second, numerous factors can inflate the cost for persons of high net worth: complexity of asset distribution, employability of

---

[10] Indeed, many people who fit the definition of high net worth don't consider themselves rich:
https://www.businessinsider.com/most-millionaires-dont-think-they-are-rich-2019-8

[11] https://www.businessinsider.com/average-cost-divorce-getting-divorced-us-2019-7

expert witnesses and the ability to hold out for what one deems a "just resolution" (when many others may need to factor-in cost as justification for settling).

Finally, because of the complex forms income and wealth can take in a high net worth situation, there are also complex ways to hide money & assets – thus often necessitating a much high degree of time and skill to uncover them so as to enable a just result for one's client[12].

This book will discuss how divorcing is different for the high income or high net worth individual. And I cannot stress enough – *especially* if you are high net worth or high income, you must consult an experienced divorce attorney at the earliest signs of trouble in your marriage. If you're the monied-spouse, you may be advised to get a post-nuptial agreement done. If you're the less-monied spouse, there may be things you can do to better

---

[12] https://www.businessinsider.com/rich-people-married-protect-money-2019-6#separate-your-forms-of-income-1

leverage yourself for custody, or a higher award of alimony, support or assets.

And while this book will highlight issues to keep in mind, it will never take the place of an individualized consultation with an attorney. Every case is different – and the advice received must be different as well.

Nevertheless, I hope this book informs you so as to aid your attorney in planning out strategy. Knowledge is indeed power – and more importantly (as my alma mater's motto is) "knowledge crowns those who use it."

DISCLAIMER

This publication is intended to be used for educational purposes only. No legal advice is being given, and no attorney-client relationship is intended to be created by reading this material. The author assumes no liability for any errors or omissions or for how this book or its contents are used or interpreted or for any consequences resulting directly or indirectly from the use of this book. For legal or any other advice, please consult an experienced attorney or the appropriate expert.

The Law Offices of David Bliven
www.blivenlaw.net

White Plains Office
19 Court St.
Suite 206
White Plains, NY 10601
(914) 468-0968

Bronx Office
3190 Riverdale Avenue
Suite 1
Bronx, NY 10463
(718) 725-9600

TABLE OF CONTENTS

i.	Foreword	3
ii.	Disclaimer	9
iii.	Table of Contents	10
1.	What Is A High Asset Or High Income Divorce In New York?	12
2.	How To Prepare for An Impending High Asset Divorce	24
3.	What Will I Get In Spousal Support Or Alimony In A High Income Divorce?	35
4.	How Are Marital Assets Divided In A High Asset Divorce?	42
5.	What Does New York Law Require Of Both Parties To Determine An Equitable Distribution Of Assets?	54
6.	What Factors Are Considered In Determining Child Custody In A High Asset Divorce?	68

7.	What Lifestyle Changes Can Someone Going Through A High Asset Divorce Expect?	76
8.	What Specific Experience and Skillset Should the Attorney I Hire for My High-Net Worth Divorce Case Have?	88
iv.	About The Author	108
v.	Testimonials	110
vi.	Index	114

CHAPTER 1

WHAT IS A HIGH ASSET OR HIGH INCOME DIVORCE IN NEW YORK?

The outcome of high income or high net-worth divorce cases is dependent in part on the geographical location where they occur – simply because incomes and wealth differ (especially between Upstate New York and Downstate New York). In general, a high-income divorce indicates that one side to the divorce has an income of at least several hundred thousand dollars more than the income of the other side, and the level of wealth is usually at least one million dollars.

What Makes High-Asset Divorces More Complex Than Standard Divorces?

A high-asset divorce will not *necessarily* be more complex than a standard divorce as same often depends on the number and form of assets. For example, if one party is simply a W-2 wage earner, only has one 401(k) account to divide, and only has one house, then that could be a simple - yet technically high-asset - divorce case.

These cases can get more complicated when restricted stock units, invested interests in companies, or partial ownership of companies is involved. There might also be multiple bank accounts where money is coming in and going out, and these accounts would need to be traced. In some cases, the assistance of a forensic accountant may be required in order to adequately opine to the attorney (and ultimately possibly to the court) the amount of income-based monies versus the amount that's simply being transferred to the account.

Does A High-Asset Divorce Take Longer and Cost More Than A Standard Divorce?

A complex high-asset divorce usually takes longer and costs more money than a standard divorce[13]. In Westchester, New York, a non-complex high-asset divorce might only take a few months, moderately complex cases may take seven months or more, and complex cases could take 11 months or more (& those times-frames are just to get the case trial-ready). Ultimately, the length of a particular case will depend on the number and type of issues that are being contested - such as asset distribution, alimony and child support, and custody or visitation.

Do I Need to Have an Attorney Review Our Prenup or Postnup Before I File for a Divorce to Ensure Everything Is Enforceable by the Courts? Isn't That the Whole Point of These Agreements in the First Place?

You should absolutely have any prenuptial or postnuptial agreement reviewed by an attorney. Yesterday, I had a client come into my office with a postnuptial agreement he and his partner had gotten off

---

[13] https://www.hg.org/legal-articles/high-net-worth-divorce-cases-unique-considerations-42301

some online website. Agreements such as this are most likely unenforceable. Among many other issues, the client's online agreement did not contain a "certificate of acknowledgement," which New York State law requires to be word-for-word pursuant to the statute. Any issue with this certificate of acknowledgement makes the agreement itself generally unenforceable.

Another issue with the online agreement was that it purported to resolve child support issues. Under New York State law and the Child Support Standards Act, you have to set forth verbatim what the presumptive calculations are for child support. If you fail to follow the statute to a T, the agreement itself is usually unenforceable.

If my client had tried to push that postnuptial agreement through court without consulting me first, the court would have rejected it - making it a complete waste of time and money.

What Are Some of The Biggest Mistakes People Make in High-Asset Divorce Cases?

Some people operate under the assumption that the only assets which will be divided are those in the account on the date of the divorce filing; as a result of this assumption, they will just transfer money out of their account prior to commencement. In reality, most attorneys will ask for the disclosure of assets at least three years prior to the date of commencement.

Savvy people may predict several years in advance that a divorce is imminent, and as a result they will start getting rid of assets prior to filing for divorce. However, even the money that is transferred or concealed several years prior to a divorce can potentially be traced. All one really has to do is pick up on the pattern of transfers out of an account. If the person transferring the money out of an account does not have an explanation as to where the money went, then the court can treat same as a form of "marital waste." In other words, the court can treat that money as if it still exists in the account.

Another big mistake people make is failing to keep track of premarital portions of various accounts and comingling property. Without thinking about it, many people will put their spouse's name on their house or place marital money into a 401(k) account. Once they start doing these things, it becomes much harder to identify what portion of an account is marital versus premarital.

What Are Some Common Questions That Clients Ask in A High Asset Divorce Case?

Many times, clients will ask what resources we are going to utilize in the course of the case. For instance, it's often helpful to have the services of a forensic accountant in high income support cases.

As another example, early in the process of a contested custody case, you should consider hiring a forensic psychological expert to help prepare for the eventual forensic interview by the court-appointed neutral. Caution should be given however that you don't want to overly prepare for such an interview. This is simply because a standard question the neutral court-assigned forensic psychological expert will ask is "who prepared you for this interview?" If they say, "my attorney had me sit with an independent forensic psychological expert and they prepared me extensively for this interview," the neutral court-assigned expert may think the interview is at least to some degree compromised by that.

So, you do want to be prepared - but not in a detailed, scripted format. I wouldn't generally advise to do a mock interview with a party but more that the independent forensic expert would talk with them about general things which are going to be discussed and how to go about answering certain questions and what to say - and what not to say.

Again, if you're going to hire an independent forensic accountant, it's better to hire one early on. If you do it that way, your expert is ready to go the minute the other side starts producing their disclosure to the attorney. You can then just scan those documents & e-mail them right over to the independent forensic accountant - who will then be able to go through them with a fine-toothed comb.

They're going to let you know whether there are holes in the person's accounts that are otherwise unexplained. They'll be able to trace certain deposits and withdrawals. For instance, many times people transfer money between accounts, either from their bank account to their credit card or from one bank account to another bank account. The forensic accountants will trace those transfers between the accounts and make sure they're all showing up - and more efficiently and more cheaply than the attorney would be able to do. Certainly, if somebody is withdrawing $10,000 from a bank account and that doesn't show up in one of the accounts, then this is a question you will need to ask them either in the interrogatories or at the depositions – but you'll want to know this well in advance of setting forth those interrogatories or conducting the deposition[14].

Is it True People in High Income or High Asset Divorces Are Choosing Mediation Over Trial?

I wouldn't necessarily say more people than in the past - mediation itself is a concept that's largely only come about in the last 10 or 20 years. Thus, it depends

---

[14] For a glossary of basic legal terms, one reference is the New York court's website:
http://ww2.nycourts.gov/divorce/glossary.shtml#I

on how far back you're setting that initial date. If one is comparing divorce cases in the '70s, '80s and even into the '90s then I may agree - but if one compares the last 10 or 15 years, I wouldn't necessarily agree. Statistically - especially in divorce cases - about 90% to 95% percent of all such cases will be settled at some point along the road. The courts & lawyers have a variety of methods for settling, *including* mediation. Nevertheless, in the cases I've handled – and I've been practicing family law for over 23 years (as of 2021) – the vast majority of them do *not* settle by going to mediation.

In my experience, it's rare for parties to opt for mediation once they hire their own attorneys. It's often more efficient to simply have the two attorneys for the husband and wife negotiate - possibly with the aid of a four-way settlement conference. That's not to say mediation doesn't work. It certainly does work when the parties go in with open minds and avail themselves of that process. It's just that usually when the parties have chosen to hire independent counsel right from the very beginning (which is again the overwhelming majority of the time), they usually just stick with their independent attorneys to negotiate a settlement.

Should I Agree to Unfavorable Terms Just to Expedite the Divorce Process?

There are many different reasons why a party should consider a settlement. I usually talk with my clients using a pure cost-benefit analysis - factoring in what they may be looking to spend in terms of my fees. If I'm representing the more-monied spouse, s/he may be contributing towards the other side's attorney's fees as well.

Let's say the issue is one of maintenance (that's New York's term for alimony), and let's say the parties are maybe a $1,000 per month apart. If you're at that point in the negotiation you can project out that maintenance will last for about three or four years. If you project that out, then a $1,000 per month difference is $36,000 over the course of 3 years. You will invariably spend $36,000+ taking the case to trial *just on your own attorney* - and that's not even talking about what you would spend (if you're the more monied spouse) on the other side's attorney's fees. Consequently, the money you're spending (by going to trial) is the maintenance money you would otherwise be getting[15].

At the end of the day, some people just want to get done with their case from an emotional/stress standpoint. It's nice to just be done and move on with your life. So, there's those considerations which come into play - and I certainly discuss all of those ancillary issues with my clients to really put it in stark contrast between settlement and taking a case to trial - and what it will cost in dollars and cents, but also what it will cost in heartache, stress, time away from your job and your family to take a case to trial.

What Are the Alternatives We Can Take Instead Of Taking Our High Asset Divorce To Trial?

Two of the most common methods are mediation or simply negotiating a settlement. You certainly don't have to take any case to trial. As stated above, about 90-

---

[15] Put another way, if you're apart by $1,000 a month and you project that out over three years you are $36,000 apart. You may be spending a large share of that $36,000 on your own attorney even if the other side contributes toward your attorney.

95% of cases settle. There is a variety of ways to negotiate a settlement, which would include four-way conferences, mediation, and consulting various experts such as forensic accountants or family counselors.

CHAPTER 2

HOW TO PREPARE FOR AN IMPENDING HIGH ASSET DIVORCE

In order to prepare for an impending high-asset divorce, I recommend people start paying off their debt because it's going to be divided anyway. Unfortunately, it's not uncommon for a court to order the debt that's in one spouse's name to be paid by that spouse - this can be problematic if debt which was generated by one spouse is not also in their name, as it can place undue debt on the other spouse.

It's also important to obtain statements pertaining to premarital contributions to one's financial accounts (e.g., investments or retirement) in order to prove what was in each spouse's financial account prior to the marriage. Depending on the length of the marriage, it could take a while to obtain this information from companies who may need to pull statements from several years prior.

When Might A Forensic Accountant's Services Be Needed in A High-Asset Divorce?

A forensic accountant might be needed in cases involving various financial accounts in which there have been many transfers in and out. A forensic accountant will also be able to determine the best ratio of division (between assets v. payment of maintenance/support) - and to trace any hidden money or hidden accounts.

Additionally, if one spouse owns their own business, the other spouse might want to hire a forensic accountant to determine the value and/or cash flow of the business[16] in order to derive the actual income of their spouse as opposed to just assuming their income is what they claim it to be. In some cases, tracing premarital contributions may not be straightforward and the assistance of a forensic accountant may be warranted. Each spouse can hire their own forensic accountant or choose to have the Court assign a neutral accountant.

In one of my cases, my client's financial accounts were about 30 years old and they really needed the assistance of a forensic accountant to step in and divvy out not only what the premarital contributions were, but also which accounts were marital versus premarital (since some accounts were rolled over into new accounts). It's certainly not impossible for an attorney to do all of this tracing, but it is *much more efficient* to retain a forensic accountant to do it, since s/he will be much more familiar with the numbers and income figures

---

[16] "Cash flow" means the difference between what a business is claiming as "income" versus what the individual owner of the business is claiming as his/her personal income.

involved - thus doing such analysis far more efficiently & cheaper than an attorney could[17]. In addition, a forensic account could testify at trial in the event there is any continued dispute with regard to the numbers.

I Trust My Ex-Spouse; Is an Investigation into Her Net Worth Necessary?

An investigation into a spouse's net worth is not necessary in all cases. If the other spouse knows their income and has seen their account assets - and if they have no reason to believe that their spouse is concealing assets – then the only thing I'd recommend is a net worth statement.

I highly recommend each party in any divorce — particularly in high-income divorces — complete a net worth statement[18]. These statements are sworn statements of one's income, expenses, assets, and debts – and thus if it's ever discovered s/he were lying on the

---

[17] https://www.hg.org/legal-articles/role-of-forensic-accountants-in-divorce-cases-35665

[18] https://www.nycourts.gov/LegacyPDFS/forms/matrimonial/NetWorthStatementFillable.pdf

statement, s/he could be held accountable and the other spouse could possibly move to reopen the divorce case.

Do We Need to Have Experts Involved in A High-Asset Divorce Case?

In a high-asset divorce case, a real estate attorney should be involved if property is being sold, but that's not usually done within a divorce case itself. In other words, if the parties settle and have a settlement agreement requiring a particular piece of property be sold, then they would independently retain real estate attorneys to facilitate the sale.

Likewise, if the settlement agreement says a business or corporation would be dissolved or sold off, then one or both parties may need to retain a business or corporate attorney to facilitate the dissolution or sale, but that would usually be done independent of a divorce case itself.

Tax experts would generally be in the guise of consulting one's own accountants on various schemes. One example (mentioned above) would be the structure of maintenance versus child support. Since maintenance is no longer deductible to the payor[19], there is less of a need for this. Nonetheless, one would still want to consult an accountant or even a forensic accountant on the best way of structuring one's settlements. In other words, an individual should determine whether there is a more financially advantageous way of structuring their settlement than what's already been put on the table by the attorney.

Indeed, forensic accountants can be helpful to discover hidden income of a business – analyzing whether the owner engaged in practices such as "deceptive payroll, underreporting income, overpaying creditors, creating fake debt, transferring assets to dummy corporations, or purchasing expensive items with secretive cash.[20]"

---

[19] https://www.irs.gov/forms-pubs/clarification-changes-to-deduction-for-certain-alimony-payments-effective-in-2019

[20] https://www.forbes.com/sites/jefflanders/2014/09/04/why-a-forensic-accountant-belongs-on-your-divorce-team/?sh=cbb862a718ab

Should We Hire Joint Forensic Accountant Experts or Hire Our Experts Individually?

Whether a joint forensic accountant or separate forensic accountants should be hired will depend on the case at hand. In my experience, the court will generally assign a neutral forensic accountant, but in "ultra-high-asset cases[21]," each individual party will likely choose to retain his/her own forensic accountant.

As an example, on one of my cases my client owned a subcontracting construction business. The business probably wasn't worth all that much on the market, but the wife was contending the possibility of hidden income. However, even if my client was hiding his income such that he was actually earning $100,000 instead of the $50,000 he claimed, the impact to potential maintenance and child support would be relatively minimal—minimal to the point that each party would not necessarily want to spend separate costs of $10,000, $15,000, or $20,000 to retain their own forensic accountant.

---

[21] As stated in the Preface, generally those involving many tens of millions in assets.

Under such circumstances, it would make better sense to retain a neutral forensic accountant.

When dealing with incomes beyond $500,000 and/or talking about dividing businesses, professional licenses[22] and/or there are many millions of dollars at stake, it makes sense for each party to retain their own independent forensic accountant—perhaps even *in addition to* a neutral forensic accountant. That way, the forensic accountant for each side could review the evaluation completed by the neutral forensic accountant and explain to the judge why s/he does or does not agree with the neutral accountant's methodology or conclusions.

---

[22] While the law changed in New York in 2016 – thus no longer making professional licenses or degree a distributable asset in themselves, they may nevertheless still be valued & factored into distribution of other assets and/or an award of maintenance. https://www.nycbar.org/get-legal-help/article/family-law/property-rights/

My Spouse Cheated on Me. Is It True That Filing for a Divorce on the Grounds of Adultery Will Make a Contested Divorce Case Harder to Win?

Yes - if you file on the grounds of adultery, you have to prove the adultery in order to proceed with your divorce case. This usually requires a grounds trial. Even if you prove your spouse cheated on you at a grounds trial, it does not actually entitle you to anything different than if you had proceeded on no-fault grounds. In other words, you will not necessarily receive more child support, spousal maintenance, or asset distribution merely because you prove adultery. Generally, filing on the grounds of adultery does not have any affect other than to terminate your marriage through a much longer and costlier divorce than one on no-fault grounds.

Are There Apps or Email Resources My Spouse and I Can Use to Communicate During a Volatile Divorce?

Yes - the court does (informally) recommend certain apps. One of the most popularly recommended apps in New York is "Our Family Wizard.[23]" This cost-effective program facilitates communication by allowing for a joint calendar and organizing discussions regarding the children by topic. When parents email each other regarding the divorce case, it's common to have one parent ask several questions and the other not respond to each of those. By organizing the conversation based on topics, "Our Family Wizard" focuses each discussion.

Additionally, the shared calendar allows parents to log the days the child is with each party, as well as keep track of school events, extracurricular activities, doctor's appointments, etc. This prevents one party from arguing the other scheduled a doctor's appointment for the child without informing them. The app funnels all communication through a third party, so if a father claims he didn't receive an email regarding a school event but the mother put it on the shared calendar, his

---

[23] https://www.ourfamilywizard.com/

problem is with the app, not with the mother. Tech support issues can't be brought up in court.

"Our Family Wizard" is certainly not the only program out there[24], but it's the one most recommended (at least in my experience) amongst Judges here in New York State.

---

[24] Soberlink (forensic alcohol testing) is one (https://www.soberlink.com/); 2Houses (https://www.2houses.com/en/), "Talking Parents" (https://talkingparents.com/home) are a couple of others.

CHAPTER 3

WHAT WILL I GET IN SPOUSAL SUPPORT OR ALIMONY IN A HIGH INCOME DIVORCE?

In New York State, there is currently a cap on income for maintenance purposes (otherwise known as alimony or spousal support) of $192,000 per year[25].

---

[25] This is as of 2021. The income cap increases by approximately $2-4,000 every two years. A useful resource on the issue is the court's website:

After plugging in each party's incomes into the presumptive maintenance calculator[26], one then deprives the "presumptive" amount of maintenance to be awarded.

In a high-income case, one of the main issues at trial will be the standard of living that the parties became accustomed to. For this, one would really need to know the spending patterns of the parties during their time of marriage. Did they go out on very expensive vacations? Did they dine at 5-star restaurants? Did they have multiple houses?

The general rule is the non-monied spouse shouldn't have to dip into her/his assets to make ends meet or maintain their standard of living. Even if one gets one million or several million dollars' worth of assets, s/he shouldn't necessarily need to spend down those assets because s/he did not receive a sufficient

---

http://ww2.nycourts.gov/divorce/MaintenanceChildSupportTools.shtml

[26]https://www.nycourts.gov/LegacyPDFS/divorce/Calculator.pdf

level of maintenance. The argument from the other spouse's perspective is, of course, they *also* shouldn't have to spend down their assets just to be able to afford a high maintenance award. They should be able to afford to pay maintenance to the other party *and* have enough money left over to pay for their own expenses.

As such, there needs to be a balancing act. Is one party, for instance, taking on debt? Is one party receiving custody of kids and thus receiving child support, in addition to maintenance? All those factors need to be thrown into the mix and only then can an appropriate level of maintenance be derived. The fact that the statute sets an income cap does not necessarily mean that you can't agree to exceed the cap. Of course, that is subject to negotiation or the discretion of a Divorce Judge, if things can't be settled.

What Factors Will Determine Spousal Support or Alimony Amount in a High Asset Divorce?

The factors that determine spousal support are the statutory factors. One would need to know the interplay of assets, child support, custody, and the standard of living. What types of restaurants would they go out to? What types of vacations would they take? What are considered "basic living expenses?" Most of that is evident from a review of the bank account statements and credit card statements. Those are the types of things that need to be looked at to determine what factors really come into play.

Nevertheless, the statutory factors[27] are as follows:

1. the age and health of the parties;
2. the present or future earning capacity of the parties, including a history of limited participation in the workforce;
3. the need of one party to incur education or training expenses;
4. the termination of a child support award before the termination of the maintenance award when the calculation of maintenance was based upon child support being awarded which resulted in a maintenance award lower than it would have been had child support not been awarded;
5. the wasteful dissipation of marital property, including transfers or encumbrances made in

---

[27] As of April, 2021.

contemplation of a matrimonial action without fair consideration;
6. the existence and duration of a pre-marital joint household or a pre-divorce separate household;
7. acts by one party against another that have inhibited or continue to inhibit a party's earning capacity or ability to obtain meaningful employment. Such acts include but are not limited to acts of domestic violence as provided in section four hundred fifty-nine-a of the social services law;
8. the availability and cost of medical insurance for the parties;
9. the care of children or stepchildren, disabled adult children or stepchildren, elderly parents or inlaws provided during the marriage that inhibits a party's earning capacity;
10. the tax consequences to each party;
11. the standard of living of the parties established during the marriage;
12. the reduced or lost earning capacity of the payee as a result of having foregone or delayed education, training, employment or career opportunities during the marriage;
13. the equitable distribution of marital property and the income or imputed income on the assets so distributed;
14. the contributions and services of the payee as a spouse, parent, wage earner and homemaker and to the career or career potential of the other party; and
15. any other factor which the court shall expressly find to be just and proper.

What Could Be Considered As "Income" When It Comes to Child Support & Spousal Support?

There are a lot of things beyond "wage income" that are considered income for support purposes. Among other things, investment income is considered income. Bonuses and overtime are considered income. If a bonus is awarded shortly after the year in which the divorce case was commenced but it was for the period of time that the person worked during their marriage, that bonus may be considered an asset and considered income for support purposes.

Rental income is also "income" for support purposes. The court also has the ability of counting things like retirement benefit or annuity distributions, fellowships, or stipends. Even non-income producing assets, like business meals or a company car can be considered as impacting the overall support amount. If someone spends money on their business but then their employer reimburses the expense, it can be claimed as income for support calculation purposes.

Beyond the above, commons forms of "income" include unemployment compensation, workers comp or disability payments, social security or veterans benefits, as well as alimony or maintenance received.

*   *   *   *

Finally, I'd refer readers over to Chapter 6 of my book "Navigating Your NY Divorce Case" for a further explanation on how maintenance is calculated in New York.

Chapter 4

How Are Marital Assets Divided In A High Asset Divorce?

Generally, property and assets are divided 50/50. This is especially true for marital assets, which are assets that accrued value during the time of the marriage.

However, it be that one spouse pays more in terms of maintenance in exchange for the other spouse waiving one or more retirement or investment accounts, or just paying a lump sum. For instance, the husband may have a lot of money in the bank and agree to give his wife more than 50 percent of it in order to buy her out of the rest of her claims.

How Important Is the Filing Date with Regard to Division of Marital Assets?

The filing date is very important with regard to the division of marital assets because it is the date on which the statute cuts off the accrual of marital assets. When I have a high-income or high-net-worth person come in for a consultation, I usually advise them to file for divorce as soon as possible so the accrual is cut off.

I also advise them to immediately cease any contributions to "marital accounts." The reason for that is, in some cases, the settlement agreement will say the non-titled spouse will share in market appreciation of accounts even post-commencement[28]. If the individual were to put money into the account, the other spouse wouldn't

---

[28] That's not the general rule, which provides that post-commencement contribution to one's own investment or retirement account is one's own "separate property." But exceptions can, and do, get made.

necessarily get the active appreciation of the account, but they may get the interest that came from that market appreciation. It may be safer to open separate financial accounts and merge them only once the divorce is complete, as doing so would make it crystal clear the accounts belong to them and that the other spouse should not share in any post-commencement market appreciation of those accounts.

How Can I Protect My Assets in A High Asset Divorce Case?

If one spouse suspects the other may do something untoward like raiding the joint account, then they should separate the account so as to prevent that (with the proviso that such divisions may be restricted after the divorce is filed).

In one case I handled, my client came to me for assistance filing for divorce and told me his wife had just taken out $400,000 from the joint account and left $200,000. Since the money had already been taken out, it became hard to get it back until we actually settled the case.

In another case I handled, the parties had just sold a condo in Manhattan and deposited approximately $250,000 into the joint account. The wife withdrew the entire amount and put it into her sole account, leaving my client with nothing. My client then filed for divorce, and we asked the Judge for 50 percent of the funds she took; the Judge responded by saying it was a trial issue and he was not going to decide on it pretrial. Effectively, this gave my client's wife a huge war chest to be able to give her attorney $250,000 to wage utter and complete war against my client, who had no money to defend himself aside from the income from his job.

One may also wish to consider retaining a firm to assist with wealth management firm[29] or an asset protection firm[30]. That said, to the degree one "hides"

---

[29] https://www.chicagobusiness.com/custom-media/wealth-divorce-roundtable.html.

[30] https://www.assetprotectionplanners.com/strategies/. Please bear in mind while I provide links to these companies, I do not necessarily endorse them – and whether one retains such a

assets or attempts to shield them from the opposing side that side may engage in "disclosure" to reveal such assets. And your attorney cannot ethically be a part of misleading the opposing side and/or the court on what assets you actually have.

I Own A Business. How Will That Impact My High Asset Divorce Case?

Among other things, your attorney would need to know whether the business started during the marriage and whether it significantly appreciated in value during the time of the marriage. If it was either started during the marriage or appreciated through active efforts during the time of the marriage, then you are talking about a marital asset.

Marital assets are subject to valuation and distribution in a divorce case. You would want to strategize with your divorce attorney and possibly hire

---

company should be done in conjunction with the advice of his/her attorney.

a forensic accountant to start planning out the best ways to structure assets within the business.

You should also be mindful that if you own your own business, that business' income will likely be considered your own income for maintenance and child support purposes.

And especially if the divorce won't be filed until long into the future, you should be mindful that "income" of a business is calculated (simply put) as "gross revenue minus (legitimate) business expenses." As such, one doesn't necessarily have an obligation to work 80-hour weeks in order to maximize income. And while the other side is entitled to argue that you're not "maximizing income" if your income is substantially reduced from prior years, this is an item in my experience which is somewhat hard to prove.

Likewise, as all business expenses are deductible from income before applying the maintenance or child support calculations, one should be mindful to maximize one's legitimate business deductions.

How Are Retirement Accounts Divided During a High Asset Divorce Case?

One needs to determine the amount of assets out there and their nature. There are many different ways accounts can be divided but one needs to determine whether there are premarital portions of those accounts, and whether there are offsets that need to be done. Offsets are a lot easier when dealing with more liquid accounts, such as IRAs, 401(k)s, or deferred compensation. They are a little harder when dealing with a pension plan because it would need to be evaluated and reduced to "present value.[31]"

A pension plan can only be awarded to a particular party upon retirement age. In the above instance, one would need to have an appraiser appraise the account and reduce it to present value by running it through an actuarial table. One may also benefit by

---

[31] To get a sense of what this means in the pension valuation context, I'd refer readers to checkout this page from one of the leading pension valuation specialists in New York: https://www.lexpen.com/valuations

having a forensic accountant or financial analyst[32] look at all the accounts to advise what would be most advantageous for the party to do. It's not as easy as looking at the dollar values of the accounts and trading one versus another because some carry transfer taxes (or taxes assessed upon one's retirement) or fees.

Is There Any Way to Prevent My Spouse from Going on A Pre-Divorce Spending Spree?

In New York State there is something called an "automatic order" which goes into effect when a divorce is filed[33]. An automatic order says neither party should take money out of (non-retirement) financial accounts[34] unless they do so "in the usual course of business for customary and usual household expenses or for reasonable attorney's fees".

---

[32] https://institutedfa.com/what-cdfa-1/

[33] https://www.nycourts.gov/LegacyPDFS/divorce/forms_instructions/Notice.pdf

[34] Retirement accounts (pensions, 401k's, IRA's, deferred compensation, etc.) have a blanket restriction – no dipping into that pool after the divorce is filed unless one has the express consent of the other party or the Judge's permission.

In a nutshell, that should restrain a party from taking $10,000 out of the joint account to have a field day at Neiman Marcus. If they do, then they have not only violated a court order, but also spent what should be considered a portion of their half of the assets in that account. For example, if the parties had $50,000 in the joint account and just before the divorce case one party took out $10,000 for unacceptable uses, then they would have just spent $10,000 of *their* $25,000, and they would be left with only $15,000 upon the division of the account's remaining assets.

Prior to the divorce being filed, if the parties have joint bank accounts or credit cards, one can move to divide those bank accounts. One can also simply go into the joint account, withdraw half of the current balance, and deposit it into a separate account[35]. You can cancel the joint credit cards[36]. There is no reason to

---

[35] After commencement of the divorce, this should be done on consent of the other spouse.

[36] If a particular card is used by the less-monied spouse and you're the more-monied spouse, be very careful to do so after notifying the other spouse of your intentions and making sure s/he has access to their own credit.

await the divorce filing. In fact, once you do file a divorce in New York State, there are certain restrictions put into place, which may prevent you from doing these things.

You should always have a consultation with a divorce attorney before moving funds or assets because there may be exceptions. One example is if your spouse is a homemaker and has no money or credit cards - cutting her off from funds may not be advisable and may provoke her to ask the court for spousal support.

How Will Our Debt Be Divided in A High Asset Divorce?

In a typical divorce, debt is divided equally. Obviously, if some of the debt with one particular party is associated just with their own expenses, you may be able to argue that some of the debt should be considered their own separate debt. It works a little differently in a high asset divorce case because a lot of the time, the high assets came about through the efforts of one party versus the other – i.e., one party makes very significant income.

Sometimes - even with high income cases - there is still credit card debt. If one party has very significant income and the other party, for instance, has very little income or no income, there may be an agreement that the debt will be paid out of assets. Or, if there is some sort of compromise on either spousal maintenance or child support, then the higher earning spouse can assume the debt[37]. Anything like that is subject to negotiation and is case specific.

Is There Any Way to Incur Your Spouse's Business Debts in a High Asset Divorce Case?

One of the things that should be done within the settlement agreement (especially in high net worth cases) is to itemize what the debt is - and the spouse who owns the business would specifically assume the business debt. There should also be an indemnification and "hold harmless clause" within the settlement agreement itself, saying that not only will the debt be in the name of the

---

[37] Example: "I'll accept $500 per month less child support is you assume the $10,000 visa debt."

business or the individual - but also if (for whatever reason) both parties are sued by a creditor, the non-debt holding spouse can counter sue the debt holding spouse for the debt and reasonable counsel fees[38].

---

[38] This latter option would be invoked if the debt-holding spouse fails to honor the indemnification clause.

Chapter 5

What Does New York Law Require Of Both Parties To Determine An Equitable Distribution Of Assets?

The first thing New York courts will look at in dividing assets is the split between marital and separate property.

The law defines "separate property" as any property that existed prior to the time of the marriage, as well as any property inherited or gifted. "Marital property" is defined as any property or assets which are either acquired or accrue "active appreciation" (or increased value) during the time of the marriage.

Both parties will need to identify what property and assets are at play - as well as debts. The equitable distribution law also extends to debts that have accrued during the time of the marriage. Generally, assets & debts are presumptively divided fifty-fifty (even more so in a medium or a long-term marriage).

What Are Considered Tangible Or Intangible Assets In A Divorce Case In New York?

In New York, the difference between a tangible and intangible asset is that a tangible asset is physical, like a vehicle or a house. Intangible assets would include money in the bank or investments. They could also include future interests in a business or a particular asset, such as future distribution of stocks.

What Is Considered A Hidden Asset In A Divorce Case?

A hidden asset would be anything one party is trying to conceal from the other party. An example would be if one party took money out of a bank account and put it in their uncle's bank account. This is not permitted. Unfortunately, some people see a divorce coming years before it is ever filed and they are able to move assets very slowly, which is harder to prove. One may then need to retain a forensic accountant to go through their expenses and then compare them to how much money they actually took out. It becomes a much more complex analysis. It is also necessary to weigh the cost of a forensic accountant against the value of the assets in question.

Do Hidden Assets In A High Asset Divorce Case Need To Be Hidden Or Could This Also Refer To A Misrepresentation Of The Value Of An Asset Or Overstating Personal Debts?

Hidden assets don't have to be literally hidden. In terms of overstating personal debts, one party can claim that their own separate debts are part of the marital debt. For example, if half of the stated debt is because one party chose to buy their new paramour an expensive diamond ring, the court will inevitably see that as their own separate purpose and remove that from the marital estate.

How Important Is the Accuracy Of The Property And Income Evaluation In A Divorce Case?

Accuracy is very important. If someone says they have a particular piece of property and it turns out they do not actually own the property or vice versa, the court can find they lied and award the non-titled spouse more assets or maintenance. In terms of income, the question of what is considered income can cause many inaccuracies. A lot of people think their income is limited to what Box 1 on their W-2 form states. However, Box 1 on their W-2 is often an inaccurate representation, even of their wage income.

Usually, we look at Box 5 on the W-2 form, which is the Medicare wages. Even that can be a misrepresentation of their overall gross income because it does not necessarily include other forms of income[39]. You also need to include things like rental income and investment income.

If One Spouse Has Been Found to Be Hiding Assets, Could This Potentially Harm His Or Her Custody Situation?

If someone misrepresented their assets and were found to have lied, it is a credibility issue. If the custody issue goes to trial, they could be cross-examined on the fact that they misrepresented the truth earlier in the process. That is an argument the other side can make to say they shouldn't be believed now.

What Evidence Can Be Used to Prove The Existence Of Hidden Assets In A Divorce Case?

The best evidence is statements or deeds. If someone claims they do not own particular pieces of

---

[39] There are certain employee benefits, such as "CAFE 125," which are above-the-line deductions and are not included in the W-2 form itself. Many times an employer will produce a separate "W-2 Summary" which then contains the additional information. See also: https://work.chron.com/calculate-total-salary-w2-10754.html

property, you can hire a private investigator to scour those pieces of property you think the person owns.

You can also have the Judge sign "information subpoenas" that would go out to particular companies. Other things can be discovered by just analyzing the financial documents you have to see whether there are transfers out to particular accounts you don't know about. They can then be asked about those items at the deposition.

Would Someone Be Able to Petition For A Modification Of Property Or Asset Division Of A Final Divorce Decree If It Is Found That Assets Were Hidden?

Whether or not such an application for modification is appropriate depends (in large part) on whether the settlement agreement states that the parties relied on certain representations made in particular documents.

Generally, settlement agreements should read that the parties have exchanged sworn net worth statements (assuming they did so) and have relied upon the representations made in those statements in making the settlement. If you have that provision in your settlement agreement and *then* you discover a piece of property or an asset the person lied about on their net worth statement, you have good grounds to reopen the divorce case. If you don't have that provision, how are you going to prove the other side lied about it?

Is There A Time Limit, After A Divorce Is Finalized In New York, To Petition for A Modification To A Final Decree, If Assets Are Later Discovered?

There is generally a statute of limitations based on fraud. It usually runs from when the fraud is actually discovered. In New York State, it is 2 years from when the fraud is discovered (or could have been discovered "with reasonable diligence").

Bottom-line, however, one should move to modify under such circumstances as soon as the alleged fraud is discovered.

Should I Or Can I Ever Hide Assets in A High Income/High Asset Divorce Case?

It is very hard to do that, especially in a high income or high asset case, because the other side will probably be doing their due diligence by tracing every single dollar of money you've taken in the first place.

One of the principal things the other side will be doing - beyond the attorney looking over the financial documents - is hiring a forensic accountant to go through financial documents. Whether a party may be successful in "hiding assets" depends (in part) on how long a time period the person has known the divorce was coming - and therefore how far in advance they have to start planning things out.

Of course, I don't advise (and I ethically cannot advise clients) to hide assets. In fact, it's the opposite – an attorney must advise clients to disclose everything they have - otherwise the attorney can get into trouble.

Certainly, I've seen cases where a party has seen a divorce case coming long before the case is actually filed. It's not so much that they hide assets, it's that they start getting rid of assets. For instance, they set up blind trusts - or I've seen other cases where instead of taking in money in checks or other traceable forms, they start taking in more money in cash. If they are an employee, they start deferring income, and/or they start deferring bonuses they've traditionally received. They may go to their boss and not put anything in writing but just simply say to their boss, "you know what? I don't want a bonus this year, give me a bonus next year (i.e., when I'm done with my divorce case)."

As long as nothing's in writing then it becomes hard for anyone to trace that. If at the end of the day the boss is friendly with the employee, while you can subpoena the boss and grill them on why they didn't give a bonus to that employee, they can just say "we just didn't give one to him/her based on company performance." Then it becomes hard to prove the other side did anything untoward in deferring cash or deferring bonuses they would otherwise receive.

Another difficult issue to uncover is when the monied-spouse owns his/her own business. S/he can then manipulate expenses (using the business account to pay personal expenses), giving loans out to employees or contractors (and have them pay it back when the divorce is over), suppressing ones efforts to earn income while the divorce is pending (so as to limit exposure to a higher maintenance/support award), re-investing the business income into the business rather than take it as personal income, and/or reaching side deals with customers to defer payments or entering barters (when that historically wasn't done). These are just a few examples – the list can be long[40].

As such, there are ways to suppress income and assets - and then it becomes up to the other side to discover same & thus prove to the Judge that at the end of the day, the Judge should consider the asset as if it still exists or that income as if it still exists.

---

[40] https://www.forbes.com/sites/jefflanders/2012/03/14/divorcing-women-heres-where-husbands-typically-hide-assets/?sh=771ca05a6579

What Are the Penalties If It Is Found That Someone Has Hidden Assets Deliberately in A Divorce Case?

Court penalties for hidden assets could include awarding a greater share of the assets to other party. The court could also award counsel fees, a greater amount of maintenance or child support, or monetary sanctions. Those sanctions may include an award of any amount the party laid out to discover the hidden assets. If someone had to hire a private investigator to discover a piece of property the other side lied about, the court could award the requesting party whatever they paid for the private investigator.

Will My Child Support or Spousal Support Be Increased If It Is Found That My Ex-Spouse Hid Assets Throughout Our Divorce?

Any property or assets can be a factor in modification of child support or maintenance, but it is only one factor.

It really goes back to whether you had a specific provision in your settlement agreement stating that the parties relied on representations made in the net worth statement in making the settlement agreement. Then, you can incorporate those net worth statements into your settlement agreement because the net worth statements will list out all of the person's assets and properties. Otherwise, there is little way to prove that the other side did not let you know they had certain properties.

Is There Anything Else Regarding Hiding Assets in A High Asset Divorce That Is Important for People To Know About?

You want to discuss with your attorney how much, realistically, those hidden assets might be worth. If they are worth a lot, then it may be worth it for you to get a forensic accountant and/or a private investigator involved. If you cannot afford this, then you need to get before the Judge right away with an application for counsel fees and expert witness fees.

It is advisable that you already contact the proposed investigator or forensic accountant, explain exactly what you want them to do, and get them to draft an affidavit - which would be included in your interim application. Then, the court can not only make an award of counsel fees but also make a separate award for expert witness fees. If you do not include a request that you want to hire experts in your counsel fee application, you'll likely have to take the money for the expert out of your counsel fees - which may drain the fees quickly.

What Are Tax Implications of a High Asset Divorce In New York?

One of the changes in the tax laws which came about very recently is that one can no longer take a tax deduction for spousal maintenance otherwise known as alimony. Consequently, any money the person now pays in terms of maintenance or child support is no longer deductible to the payor and no longer included as income to the payee. The practical implication of this is it now makes sense to pay a lower amount of maintenance and transfer more assets simply because the person is going to be getting the money anyway.

As an example, let's say the assets are in the form of retirement assets. When you go to retire, you're going to have to pay taxes on that money - and if you no longer have that money because you transferred it to your spouse, then guess who gets to pay the taxes on that money? Your spouse - when they go to retire. It may thus be advisable - if the other side will accept it - to try transferring a greater share of a 401(k) or a pension (or other retirement) to the less monied spouse in exchange for a much lower (or even eliminated) maintenance amount.

Chapter 6

What Factors Are Considered In Determining Child Custody In A High Asset Divorce?

Invariably the parties in a high-income case have relatively more to spend litigating the case. Custody issues are extremely expensive issues to go through. One may need to pay for a forensic psychological evaluation or even a second opinion of that evaluation, plus pay the attorneys to do a contested child custody case.

It's not unheard of for cases like that to cost $200,000 or more. For some people who make a high amount of income and have many millions of dollars in assets, that amount is not going to faze them (especially when considering it's effectively an investment in the children's futures). One needs to negotiate and consider other factors, in terms of the likelihood of success and what going through a custody case will do to the kids.

Early on in the process, one should consider retaining an independent forensic psychologist – particularly if either side has a mental health issue, or there are any other issues a forensic psychologist could potentially opine on (e.g., domestic violence, anger management, child abuse, parental alienation, etc.).

One may also consider retaining a social worker expert – who may opine on such issues as "battered women's syndrome" or various structures of visitation[41]. They can also draft a psycho-social

---

[41] https://www.expertinstitute.com/resources/insights/family-law-expert-witness-introduction-family-law/.

background of the family – which may be helpful if one is attempting to demonstrate to the court why visitation should be restricted – and/or why joint custody is not feasible.

Finally, as the case gets closer to trial, one may consider retaining a "witness preparation" coach.

How Can Clients Who Are Very Involved in Their Work Protect Their Custody Rights?

If someone is travelling a lot or doesn't have the time to go through a contested custody case, then one really needs to discuss with his/her attorney whether it makes sense to go through the contested custody case. Availability to the child is a factor the Judge can consider against him/her. If one parent has more availability, that parent is much more likely to be awarded custody. If there is a high disparity of income, you may not only be paying for your lawyer, you'll also likely be spending money on your spouse's lawyer as well. Those are all things to throw into the "consideration bucket."

You're best advised to keep a paper-trail with the opposing party, as well as a timeline of key events. An example of a timeline follows:

Date	Key Event	Link to Evidence
1/23/21	Returned Junior with a bruise	1/23/21 Pic
2/23/21	Dropped Junior off 30-min late	E-mail exchange confirming same
3/6/21	Threatened me "I'll pay" if I don't agree to his demands	Voice-recording
3/16/21	Exhibited signs of depression	Video record

How Do We Narrow Issues for Litigation or Trial In A High Income Divorce Case?

One really needs to zero in on which issues are in contention and which issues are not. That said, I am wary of resolving only certain issues and leaving other issues open. For instance, I'm often reluctant to settle the custody and visitation issues before one settles the financial issues, especially payment of maintenance and child support.

In some cases, wanting to give up one's ability to sue for custody of one's children is predicated upon the amount of support s/he may have to pay. As such, knowing what they need to pay may factor into whether they would want to settle on custody. Leaving the support amount as an open issue while resolving custody and visitation oftentimes takes that out of the mix. In such instance, they'll be giving up something which may potentially be used as leverage[42] and vice versa.

As a further example, if the mother resolves the child support and maintenance issue while leaving the custody issue open, she may have compromised on the amount of support and settle for a lower amount than one would otherwise agree to (if one prevailed at a custody trial and got sole custody). As a result, in many cases global settlements work better for both parties.

I Have the Financial Resources to Relocate My Children. Should I Do So Now or Wait Until There's a Written Agreement Defining Our Temporary Custody Before the Divorce Is Final?

You should not generally relocate the children to another residence absent at least a temporary agreement to that effect. The other side may consent

---

[42] Allow me to clarify: one should never use children as pawns in a game to get more – or pay less – in support. One should only contest custody if one truly wants the children to live with oneself. The point here is simply that if one eventually pays so much in support to the custodial parent that one will not be able to maintain an adequate house or lifestyle for the children, perhaps it's then better to have the children live with you.

to relocation if you're not moving far away in terms of distance and if they're not contesting custody. Otherwise, relocation should await a final resolution in the case. If there is an urgent reason for you to relocate sooner rather than later (such as escaping a domestic violence situation), then you should generally make an application to the divorce judge and get court approval first[43].

My Separation Has Been Volatile. I Need to Move Out Now. Could My Spouse Use This as Leverage If I Move Out Without My Children?

The answer is yes. If you move out without your children, you're giving *de facto* custody to your spouse. Only very rarely would I advise a client (who wants custody of their children) to move out without bringing the children with them. If you do not have consent to bring your children with you, that's an issue

---

[43] Please checkout Chapter 3 of my book "Navigating Your NY Family Court Case" for more on relocation issues.

of contest, which should be brought before the divorce judge sooner rather than later[44].

* * * *

As this book is primarily focused upon the financial issues involved with high net worth divorce cases, if your case involves contested custody or visitation issues, then I'd invite you to checkout Chapter 8 of my book "Navigating Your NY Divorce Case" or Chapters 1 and 2 of my books "Navigating Your NY Family Court Case.

---

[44] One exception is if one is fleeing from a domestic violence situation.

CHAPTER 7

WHAT LIFESTYLE CHANGES CAN SOMEONE GOING THROUGH A HIGH ASSET DIVORCE EXPECT?

A lot of times people get used to a high lifestyle when the two parties are living together and they have the benefit of either a very high-income spouse - or perhaps *both* spouses are earning a high amount and therefore the household has $500,000+ and the parties budget out their expenses accordingly. Accordingly, they have a relatively high mortgage, they send the kids to private school, they both buy expensive cars, they hire nannies (or au pairs), etc. Once they budget everything out, you're talking about monthly expenses that would net $10,000, $15,000, $20,000 or more in a month. That's all fine when the parties are living under one roof – but when the households are divided, even a high amount of income only goes so far.

What happens when the parties physically separate is that now each party has to maintain separate household expenses. It's often the concern of the spouse moving out of the marital residence that they'd be able to move into a residence which will be suitable for the child(ren). In other words, if the kids are used to living in a marital residence that's relatively upscale, then they arguably got used to that type of living. Are they realistically going to be fine with going over to Dad's new two-bedroom condo in Yonkers? Probably not. So, it's a legitimate concern of the spouse moving out of the marital residence – and after payment of maintenance and child support – will be able to afford a decent place on his or her own.

It's recommended to project out what one's expenses will be once one does move out of the marital residence - perhaps with the assistance of a forensic accountant (or financial planner[45]). I usually tell them right at the beginning of the case, if you're still living in the marital residence, you then need to start pricing out housing situations elsewhere. Start shopping now, because that may impact the amount of maintenance and child support you're going to be able to afford to offer to the other side.

How Can A High Asset Divorce Impact My Business and Other Stakeholders Involved in The Business?

It depends on whether you have partners in your business. A lot of times if there's a business that was started during the marriage the non-titled spouse will be entitled to a share of the business value, so that business can have a price tag essentially put on it. The owner of the business may have to pay a share of the value to the

---

[45] https://institutedfa.com/learning-center/what-cdfa-professional/.

non-titled spouse - and depending on the amount of assets the business has, it could theoretically be a significant hit on the business. The other way it would impact the businesses is if the business itself would have to turn over a trove of financial documentation - and the consequent time involved in doing so.

A lot of times in those cases which involve valuation of a business, a forensic accountant is assigned (or retained) to help value the business - and therefore the titled spouse will have to produce mounds of documentation to the forensic accountant. It's usually advisable for the titled spouse who owns a business to hire an independent forensic accountant to assist them with the process of producing the necessary documents to the court-assigned neutral forensic accountants.

I've seen the following happen way too often: the owner of the business will just keep operating the business - whether it's a medical practice, real estate practice, etc. – while the divorce is ongoing. They are going to be out treating their patients, showing houses etc. and they're not going to have time left over at the end of the day to pull up a U-Haul to their office and load boxes of documents into the truck & get them over to the court-assigned neutral accountant.

Under those circumstances they would benefit by having their own accountant to take in the list of documents that the court-assigned neutral accountant wants. The two accountants can then talk to each other and coordinate efforts to make sure the court-assigned neutral accountant gets everything they need to do their analysis for the court and for the attorneys.

If it's just left to the titled spouse to do all that, it's more likely the case will be delayed simply because they're not going to have the time. The court-assigned neutral accountant will keep getting back to them over and over again with another list of documents that they have to produce because they didn't produce enough documents on their first request.

What Advice Do You Give Clients About Communicating with Their Ex in A Divorce?

This depends principally on whether domestic violence has been an issue in the case or allegations of domestic violence have arisen. If there have been, I usually advise them to limit communication. If there is an order of protection already in place that bars communication, then it's obvious they can't have any communication.

If that's not the case, then it's not bad to talk to their soon-to-be ex-spouse about settlement terms. A lot of times parties can just discuss amongst themselves after they've had certain discussions with their own attorneys about numbers and where they want to end up. Sometimes "kitchen table discussions" go further than four-way settlement conferences (ones with the attorneys present). Once attorneys get involved, we must advise our clients in a certain way and some attorneys overlook the "I just want to be done with this" factor. That can have a certain amount of value independent of just the dollars and cents.

Sometimes when the parties both talk to each other about the case, they'll say at the end of the day, "these attorneys are here to make money," and that's true. Attorneys *are* in this business to make money for themselves principally. Secondly, if I can do a good job for people and leave people happy and service them and get them on with their lives, that's great. I'm not discounting that at all but at the end of the day - just like with a doctor, an accountant, or a mental health professional - we're all here to make money. If I can get a case done and only make $5,000 (or less), fine by me - I'll move on to my next case.

That was the situation with a high-income case I recently settled where the parties at least initially were gearing up to have a drawn-out contested custody battle. The case settled when I sat my client down and I said:

> **there's two directions this case is going to go. One way is we're going to go to trial and somebody is going to get custody and somebody is going to get visitation. Either way, you are looking at spending at least $100,000 just on my fees alone. That doesn't count the**

fees of the forensic accountant, it doesn't count the fees of the attorney for the children, it doesn't count the fees for the forensic psychological evaluation which in the Greater New York City area, may cost about $20,000+ in itself. At the end of the day if you can arrive at a doable settlement agreement, you hash out what the numbers are going to be, you hash out what the access arrangements are going to be, something that you could live with, at the end of the day is that what has more meaning to you? If you can get out of this only spending $5,000 or $10,000 as opposed to $100,000?

When I said it like that, he said "I'll discuss things with my wife." The case had been pending for several months with no movement whatsoever, but within one week he got back to me and said "I spoke to my wife. We're going to settle. We've already discussed all the terms of the settlement and I'll send you an email that gives you a bullet point list of everything that we settled on." At the end of the day the client was happy, I was happy & I moved on to my next case. I didn't make $100,000 off that case but I had a happy client. A lot of times what benefits me as an attorney is to have those frank discussions with the clients and say "this is realistically what it's going to cost you. Do you want to jump in that deep pool or not?"

Are There Ways We Can Protect the Privacy of Our Divorce from Social Media or Even Press?

In the state of New York, divorce cases are presumptively confidential, which means that parties' names generally cannot be searched online to find court documents. That said, if someone has celebrity status or is concerned about the public's ability to search the court system website by their name to come up with any lawsuits, that person can file an application with the court to receive permission to make the divorce filing anonymous. In those cases, the court uses the parties' initials for court reference so their names are not searchable by members of the press or the general public.

In terms of social media, it is usually only the parties who might be posting information about each other online. If one party wants to prevent the other from posting online, they would need to get a stipulation immediately from the other side's counsel to bar both parties from posting any information or documentation about their divorce case online[46]. This would also prevent any third party from doing so. If something has already been posted, it can be brought to the attention of the divorce judge.

If one is worried about cyber-stalking, then one may give thought to engaging a tracking company such as Family Docket[47]. In some cases – depending on the nature of the post, social media postings can constitute a crime of "unlawful dissemination or publication of an intimate image," harassment or stalking.

---

[46] For a good article on the do's & don't of social media during a divorce, checkout: https://www.divorcemag.com/blog/social-media-use-during-divorce-why-you-shouldnt-engage.

[47] https://www.familydocket.com/.

Is It Possible in a High-Profile Divorce to File for a Divorce Under Anonymous Caption and Have All of Our Public Records Labeled Anonymous or Sealed? What Are the Pros and Cons of Doing So If This Is an Option?

As discussed earlier, you can file a divorce case under an anonymous caption. To request an anonymous caption, you would have to make an application to the court for them to accept the anonymous caption. Depending on the court, they may accept a cover letter, or may request a more formal application.

The biggest "con" in this situation is being required to complete a formal application and file a motion, which increases court costs. In the case of high-profile divorces - involving either celebrities or public figures - cost is usually not a factor, so it's advisable to take the extra step for anonymity.

The "pro" would be preventing your names from being searchable online regarding the divorce case. The State of New York has "E-Courts" on their court system website, which allows members of the press (or anyone else for that matter) to monitor whether anything is filed by a celebrity or public figure. You can only avoid the press locating your divorce suit if you're filing anonymously.

Is It True That If We Drag Our Divorce Case to Trial, Everything Will Become Public Record?

No - in New York State, all divorce cases are confidential in nature, so whether your case goes to trial or stays pre-trial, everything is protected from public disclosure - although again parties names themselves may be reflected in the "E-Courts" system.

In theory, if a member of the press somehow got wind of the divorce filing, they do have the ability to file a motion to be able to know about the circumstances of the divorce or even sit in on the trial. That being said, the parties would also have the ability to oppose that motion, and then the judge can rule on whether any members of the press or public would be allowed to view the trial.

Chapter 8

What Specific Experience and Skillset Should the Attorney I Hire for My High-Net Worth Divorce Case Have?

Not all attorneys are created equal - simply because attorneys vary by experience and by knowledge. An attorney who's been in practice 20 or 30 years certainly has a lot more experience than an attorney who's just graduated from law school or even one with 5-10 years of experience. With a high-net-worth or high-income divorce case, you should generally aim to hire the more experienced attorneys (those with at least 20 years of practice). The sweet spot of experience is between 25-35 years' experience – if any attorney has more than 40 years' experience, s/he is likely in their mid-60's and thus nearly the age at which one won't likely have the energy necessary for a high stakes case[48].

Good attorneys also invariably specialize or concentrate their practice in one particular field versus another. You wouldn't want to hire a personal injury or criminal law attorney to handle your high-income divorce. Only an attorney who concentrates most of their practice (if not all) on divorce law and family law will bring you the confidence of him/her being well-versed in this area of law. Each attorney has a limited number of hours they can spend at the office, as well as a limited number of hours to keep up with the law and the various case law interpretations coming down

---

[48] This is obviously painting with a broad brush – merely because a person is in their mid to high 60's doesn't mean they can't handle complex matters – after all, we've had recent Presidents in their 70's.

from the appellate courts. If an attorney's time is divided between five or six different areas of law, they won't be able to know as much about one area of law as an attorney who solely concentrates on that one area. You should take that into consideration when hiring an attorney for your divorce case.

What Other Professionals Should I Consider Consulting Along with My Attorney to Evaluate My High-Net-Worth Divorce?

You would certainly want to consider consulting a forensic accountant, who would be able to tell you things like what is more advantageous for you to offer in terms of certain transfers of assets and property, as well as what's more advantageous in terms of transfers of property versus payment of child support and maintenance. A forensic accountant can advise you better than an attorney can in terms of the tax consequences of any given settlement scenario, so you should work in conjunction with that forensic accountant and your attorney to propose several different settlement scenarios.

Let's say you have a grouping of properties or assets and want to know, "If I transfer property A and C and asset portfolio 1, 5, and 7 to my spouse, is that more advantageous versus paying a higher amount of maintenance and child support?" You can interplay the properties, the assets, the maintenance, and the child support in a wide variety of ways. Ultimately, you want that forensic accountant to weigh in on what - on a long-term basis or even a short-term basis - is going to be more advantageous to you in terms of taxes and financial planning.

You may also wish to consider retaining an investigator – especially if there are any issues with hidden income or assets. As stated above, you may wish to also consider retaining a forensic financial planner[49].

---

[49] You should also refer to the prior chapters in this books, as I've made numerous other suggestions above on retaining experts.

Additionally, you may consider retaining the services of a domestic violence expert (if that's an issue), or a custody or divorce coach[50].

Finally, consider hiring a vocational expert if maintenance (a/k/a "alimony") is an issue & it may be alleged the spouse requesting maintenance is suppressing his/her income.

What Impact Do Assets Have When Hiring an Attorney in A High Net Worth Divorce?

For starters, if you don't have substantial income (well over $200,000+) or assets (over $1 million), then you may not be considered a high net worth case. Regarding the assets, you also want to look at whether they are simple or complicated. A typical family may own a house, have retirement assets, have particular investment vehicles, and if it's not all that complicated then perhaps an average divorce attorney could handle the case. Nevertheless, the more complicated the investments or retirement, then an attorney who is

---

[50] https://divorcesupporthelp.com/.

particularly skilled in those issues will most likely need to be hired (especially if somebody owns a business or professional practice).

A client should interview their potential attorneys[51] along the lines of how many high net worth divorces they have done. Do they have any particular qualifications that would essentially aid them in a high net worth divorce case? For example, in New York and a few other states, the American Academy of Certified Financial Litigators[52] or "CFL" is a designation a growing number of attorneys (including myself) have. Attorneys with the CFL designation specialize in divorce work with high net worth or high-income divorces. The certification demonstrates that the attorney has studied extensively, and at the end of the study has taken a relatively rigorous examination to get their certification. Having this certification indicates the attorney has a particular specialized knowledge in the

---

[51] https://www.brides.com/questions-to-ask-before-hiring-a-divorce-attorney-1102832.

[52] https://aacfl.org/.

financial field, which would come into play in a complicated scenario as outlined earlier.

Is It Important for A High Net Worth Divorce Attorney to Have Keen Insight On Business Valuations, Equitable Division Of Real Estate, Stock Options, IRAs, Etc.?

It *is* important for a high net worth divorce attorney to have keen insight on business valuations, equitable division of real estate, stock options, IRAs, and more. It's essential because the attorney has to know how to identify certain issues. It also takes a certain base of knowledge to even understand the issues which apply to certain circumstances, and to determine the type of settlement proposal that would better suit their client.

Many attorneys in high net worth or high-income cases will hire a forensic accountant to assist them with the process of presenting their client's case. However, if the attorney does not have a certain base of knowledge on the financial issues, they're not as likely to understand what the forensic accountant is trying to explain to them, and more importantly, they are not going to know how to best present that information at a potential trial.

The forensic accountant can testify, but at the end of the day, it's the attorney who's responsible for presenting the evidence to the Judge in a manner he or she can comprehend. If the attorney doesn't comprehend it, then it would really beg the question: how would they be able to present it in a way that a Judge would comprehend it?

How Important Is Experience in High Net Worth Divorce Cases?

Experience is very important in a high net worth divorce case. Generally, the more experience one has in high income or high net worth divorces, the better off they are.

One can compare the extremes. For instance, if you have somebody who is fresh out of law school who's never handled a divorce before (let alone a high net worth divorce), as opposed to an attorney with 20 or 30 years of experience who's handled hundreds of high income or high net worth divorces, then one would obviously see the difference between the two.

What Service Should I Expect from An Experienced Attorney in High Net Worth Divorces?

It starts right at the beginning. An attorney who specializes in high net worth or high-income divorces will have a computerized practice management system (such as Time Matters, Clio, Atticus, etc.) which helps them keep everything on track in terms of their client's particular case. They'll have paralegals dedicated to their case that have a relatively low caseload.

In my firm, for example, although I'm a solo practitioner, I have two full-time paralegals - each with a caseload of approximately 30 to 35 cases. That means my paralegals can stay on top of the cases to better present the case for settlement or trial. In addition, my office has a dedicated intake specialist whose job is to answer the phones and do administrative tasks around the office. In turn, that frees up the paralegals to concentrate on the grunt work of the cases.

Now, if a solo practitioner or a relatively small firm only has one employee working for them, and they are a jack of all trades (i.e., doing a little bit of everything), then his/her paralegal or legal assistant isn't going to have enough time to adequately prepare a case - as compared to an attorney who has either one or two paralegals that concentrate solely on paralegal work.

I think that it's a matter of asking any potential attorney about their caseload. How many cases do you currently have? How many paralegals do you have dedicated to you? These questions also apply if you go to a big firm. It's a mistaken assumption to believe that if you have a high income or high net worth case, you need to hire a firm with 100+ lawyers in a gleaming office tower in Manhattan or Westchester.

Here's the problem with that belief: in an area of law done by the billable hours - such as divorce and family law - every attorney will have to have their own caseload in order for any firm to afford the rent which comes with a luxury office building. With family law, unless the attorney has a caseload of 50, 60, 70 cases, one would really wonder how that firm is able to make ends meet if they're specializing in divorce and family law. And going back to the large firm - if you hire a large law firm with 100 or 200 lawyers, each lawyer is going to have their own caseload of 50, 60, 70 cases. Consequently, that caseload is comparable to a solo practitioner's caseload.

You also should ask your potential attorney: do they specialize? Are they concentrated on one area of law or at most two or three areas of the law? Or are they a jack of all trades? For a high income and high net worth case, you want to make sure your attorney is a specialist who concentrates their practice in divorce and family law. Maybe they do one or two other areas of law, but the other areas are a relatively small percentage of their overall caseload. The vast majority of their cases - perhaps 70%, 80%, 90%, or 100% of their caseload - should be divorce and family law.

In other words, on caseload alone, there is generally no advantage in hiring a large law firm as opposed to a small law firm or solo practitioner. In reality, you want to go further and ask any particular attorney - whether they're a solo practitioner, a small firm, or a 500-attorney firm: what is your caseload? Do you have a dedicated paralegal? If so, what is that paralegal's caseload? Some law firms that have a 100 or more attorneys will make it seem as if they're bringing their entire firm to concentrate on your case if you hire them. That's not the way it works. Once you are out the door, your file goes into one attorney's office, and s/he is likely the sole, dedicated attorney to the case. Very rarely will you have a case where two attorneys will be working equally on the case.

Also, the paralegals in the much bigger firms may not have a caseload that is less than the caseload of a paralegals in small firms (or solo practitioners). For instance, I know one firm in particular that has several paralegals who number about half the amount of attorneys - consequently, each paralegal will have at least twice as many, if not three times as many cases as the particular attorney. Thus, if an attorney has a caseload of 60 or 70 cases, one paralegal in that firm will have a caseload of 100-150+ cases.

If the attorney or their paralegal is overwhelmed with cases – and you have a high income or high net worth case - the time that firm can devote to preparing your case may not be sufficient. If you have a relatively complex issue, it will take time to sift through all the documents that are going to be involved in your case (e.g., all the years of financial records from various accounts), and then to be able to formulate a settlement proposal or prepare the case for trial requires dedication.

At the end of the day, if the attorney has 80+ cases and his/her paralegal has many more cases than that - or they don't even have a paralegal dedicated to your case - they're just not going to be able to devote as much time to preparing your case properly. Those are some of the questions you should be asking your potential attorney whether they are a solo practitioner, a small firm, or an associate or partner of a firm that has 500 or more attorneys.

Should I Take Suggestions from Friends and Family In Hiring A High Net Worth Divorce Attorney?

There is nothing wrong with taking suggestions from friends and family when hiring a high net worth divorce attorney as long as they're good suggestions. The questions should remain the same even though a friend or family member suggests an attorney. You have to ask that attorney: do you specialize in divorce law and family law? What is your caseload like? Do you have a dedicated paralegal? What is their caseload like? In other words, are they going to have the time to properly prepare the case? How many cases have they done which are high net worth or high-income cases?

Now, attorneys are restrained based on ethical rules. They cannot discuss specific cases (unless they have been publicly reported cases) of high net worth or high-income cases due to confidentiality. That said, we can certainly discuss with any particular client or potential client the number of cases we've done, the types of assets that were involved, the types of incomes that were involved, and the type of success one had on those types of cases. Therefore, it's one thing to get the referral from a family or friend, but you also want to make sure the referred attorney knows what they're doing when it comes to your particular case.

Should I Look at Testimonials & Online Reviews When Researching an Attorney?

You *should* look at testimonials and online reviews when researching an attorney. That's a factor you should consider - but it's only one factor amongst many different factors that you should consider.

In other words, if the attorney you're looking at doesn't even have a website, you should ask: why is that? Perhaps the attorney gets a lot of referrals from word of mouth - but on the other hand, in the 21st century, I'd be concerned about any attorney who doesn't have a website. At the same time, look at websites like AVVO[53] or Google, both of which are two of the top sites in terms of attorney reviews. If the attorney you're looking at doesn't have any online

---

[53] https://www.avvo.com/.

reviews or only very few online reviews, those are questions to ask the attorney. Therefore, how can you as a potential client independently verify whether their clients have actually liked them or not - and are satisfied with their services?

On the other hand, you should be wary of attorneys who seemingly have hundreds of positive reviews. I know of a few law firms in the Bronx or Westchester area which have 300-400+ mostly positive reviews on their Google Review Page. Whereas almost all of the other attorneys in this field may have roughly 20-40 reviews in total. So, as a potential client, you should be concerned about that in terms of whether they are paying a service to do their reviews for them. Unfortunately, in this world, some people are dishonest, and the dishonesty can float into the area of attorneys. I cannot name names, but I know some attorneys out there hire companies to do fake positive reviews for them.

They will simply farm out and pay a high school student or college student to go on Google to give a particular attorney a positive review with a script on what to say. The attorney will take out a subscription and pay around $50 to $100 a month to get a few new positive reviews which seem like it's coming from actual clients - except they're not. They're coming from this sham company who's just paying some college students to write fake positive reviews. On Google's end, it's almost impossible to police. They don't circle back to the attorney and verify whether these are actual positive reviews. It then becomes a matter of the potential client doing independent research and asking that particular attorney the right questions.

If all other attorneys have 20-50 online reviews, but the attorney one is visiting has 200-300+ reviews, don't hesitate to ask: why is it that you have 10 times the reviews of all other attorneys in this field? Are you paying a service to do these reviews for you? Also, you can go through a random sample of their reviews and ask about a case s/he had with that firm. You can say, "this person gave you a review, tell me about his/her case?" Or "I see *Jane Doe* gave you a positive review a couple months ago & you just recently finished her case. Tell me a little bit about her case?"

If the attorney gives you a blank look, then you know they're lying to you, and you should turn around and walk quickly out of their office.

Do I Need to Have an In-Person Consultation Prior To Hiring An Attorney?

You should definitely have an in-person consultation with a potential attorney[54]. That's my standard operating procedure. There are certain subjective qualifications that you are going to get. You can read online about the attorney. How many years have they been in practice? You can also email them and ask about the number of high net worth cases that they have worked with. You can read their online reviews.

However, there are certain things that you just can't pick up on from a phone call or their website. Consulting with the attorney in person can help you

---

[54] Though post-pandemic, a lot of attorneys (myself included) are accommodating virtual (FaceTime, Zoom, etc.) consultations.

determine whether you feel comfortable with him or her. If you go into their office, is it completely messy? Are there papers strewn all over the place? Do you have the feel that this is the high-end law firm you would want it to be for your high net worth divorce case?

Is their office in a nice neighborhood? Is it in a nice building? When you walk in, is it a calming experience where you don't feel rushed? Is the staff friendly to you? Do they appear rushed in the consultation - and do they give you as much time as you need to answer all of your questions? Those types of affirmations are only obtained when you meet with the attorney face to face.

What Can I Learn from the Attorney in The First Consultation In My Het Net Worth Divorce Case?

In the first consultation, you should not only expect to have your questions answered, but you should also have the attorney walk you through the divorce process.

The attorney should also talk about their strategy for your case to help you with particular financial division, asset distribution, maintenance, child support issues, and all other issues should be addressed. If you are the one seeking maintenance and child support, you should talk about the strategies that will maximize those amounts. If you are the one defending against those claims, your attorney can advise on the strategies that will minimize maintenance and child support, if that's your aim. Those issues should all be discussed at the initial consultation.

*   *   *   *

Bottom-line: preparation is key! Ideally, you'll want to begin your preparation for your high net worth divorce case long before it's filed – from selecting experts, to choosing the right attorney, and to begin "getting your affairs in order" to help ensure the best result possible for you[55].

---

[55] https://www.huffpost.com/entry/40-secrets-only-divorce-a_b_8602766

ABOUT THE AUTHOR

David Bliven graduated with honors from Syracuse University in 1993 with a B.A. in Sociology. He went on to serve as a statistician with the NYS Commission on City Court Judicial Reallocation with the Office of the Deputy Chief Administrative Judge. He then attended New York Law School where he graduated in 1997 with honors and ranked within the top 15% of his class.

Shortly after graduating, he served as a prosecutor for nearly 3 years with the NYC Administration for Children's Services. While at ACS he prosecuted child support, child abuse & neglect and foster care cases on behalf of the City of New York.

After leaving the prosecutor position, Mr. Bliven opened his present practice in 2000. His practice is currently devoted 100% to Divorce & Family Court cases.

Mr. Bliven has an "AV" rating from Martindale-Hubbell (the highest possible rating in both Legal Ability & Ethical Standards), a perfect 10.0 rating from Avvo ("Superb" rating) and is listed in the "Super Lawyers" directory by Thompson Reuters (a distinction given to less than 5% of all attorneys in each field of practice). He is also a "Certified Financial Litigator" and was honored as a "Super Lawyer" for the NY Metro & Westchester area by *Westchester Magazine* in their October, 2019 issue.

Mr. Bliven also authors "Cases That Help" - an annual caselaw newsletter distributed to Family Court Assigned Counsel panels throughout the State of New York, and his articles have been published in the New York Law Journal, Nolo.com and Westchester Lawyer Magazine.

TESTIMONIALS

- Anonymous: "During a time, when it seemed as my life was about to fall apart, Mr. Bliven was there to make sure I was protected. Mr. Bliven was there to make sure every "T" was crossed and every "I" was dotted. He made sure I was entitled to my fair share. When children are involved in a divorce, I wanted to make sure they were taken care of for the foreseeable future. Mr. Bliven made it his duty to fight for me when he felt I deserved more retribution. He fought tooth and nail for the needs of my children as well as for me. During a time when things looked bleak, Mr. Bliven made sure my legal and financial needs are taken care of. When beginning this venture, I was scared that I would walk off of this with only my "shirt", but Mr. Bliven made it his job to make sure I was able to resume my life without looking back. I want to thank Mr. Bliven and I would recommend him to anyone who is and is thinking about filing for a divorce."

- Jonathan: "Mr. Bliven came very highly recommended to me by a friend who used to practice family law and had transitioned into other areas of legal practice. I was not disappointed. Mr. Bliven was thoroughly knowledgeable and highly attentive as he helped me smoothly resolve complex child support matters involving international issues of competing jurisdictions. Having had a number of attorneys in the course of my divorce and child custody/support matters over the last 18 years, I believe I am experienced to know that Mr. Bliven is a top family law expert."

- Lou: "Mr. Bliven represented me in a child support case. I was very pleased with the services provided by Mr. Bliven. He is professional, courteous, and knows his stuff! I am completely gratified with the outcome of my case. Thanks to Mr. Bliven's knowledge of family law. Mr. Bliven kept me up to date on all matters pertaining to my case and his billing is fair and accurate for the work he puts into the case. I would certainly recommend him to anyone that is seeking a topnotch lawyer in the area family court."

- Teri Colon: "Although I have not met with Mr. Bliven yet. I contacted his office on a Friday of a Holiday Weekend. His office's response was immediate and I was treated with respect as if I was already a client. His staff took the time to email me immediately and when I called I was given an appointment that accommodates my schedule. Custody matters are very sensitive and clients can be emotional. It was a relief to speak with someone who was not only professional and courtesy, but also showed genuine concern. I look forward to my consultation with Mr. Bliven."

- Ariane: "Mr. Bliven was knowledgeable, informative, and an incredible strategist. He used all of my legal rights to defend me in my case and was extremely professional to work with. I can't thank him enough for his ability to use our rights as law-abiding citizens and to get the job done. David consulted with me on all motions before revealing them to the court or to any other parties. For this I thank him and am grateful for his diligence in representation."

- Gregg: "Although I subscribe to a legal plan through my union (I'm a teacher), I decided to retain Mr. Bliven based on our initial consultation. He seemed much better versed than the less expensive "plan" attorney I spoke to in the child support matter I brought to him. Mr. Bliven scanned the paperwork I brought with me to the consultation and immediately developed a strategy using various points of law. Mr. Bliven kept in constant contact with me and "cc'd" me on all correspondence he and my ex-wife's attorney had via email or hard-copy. Mr. Bliven's courtroom demeanor was just as I had hoped it would be; vocal and on point. Ultimately, my ex-wife and I reached a fair compromise that did not follow the default percentages NY State dictates. I would definitely retain again should the need arise."

- A Satisfied Client: "Navigating family court for personal reasons can be quite intimidating, even for folks who have interfaced with court officers and judges for professional purposes. That said, Bliven was nothing short of extremely knowledgeable, courteous and very attuned with the emotional experience that comes with the process. I highly recommend Bliven if you are seeking consultation and representation with a child support and/or custody case!"

****

More Testimonials may be found on David Bliven's website (http://www.blivenlaw.net/Testimonials.shtml) and at Avvo (https://www.avvo.com/attorneys/10463-ny-david-bliven-952796.html#client_reviews).

* * * *

If you appreciated the information given to you in this book, Mr Bliven would appreciate a review of the book on Amazon and/or a Google review:

https://g.page/law-offices-of-david-bliven-933/review?rc

INDEX

C

child support · 66

D

de facto custody · 74
debt · 51
domestic violence · 74

E

equitable distribution law · 55

F

financial investment
　retirement account · 25
forensic accountant · 26
forensic psychological evaluation · 68

H

high income spouse · 76
high net-worth divorce · 12
high-asset divorce · 13

M

Marital property · 55

P

postnuptial agreement · 14
premarital contributions · 25
prenuptial · 14

R

Rental income · 40

retirement assets · 66

S

settlement agreement · 52

spousal maintenance · 66

spousal support · 37

T

tangible and intangible asset · 55

W

W-2 wage earner · 13

Notes

Made in the USA
Las Vegas, NV
09 December 2024